The Cynic

...their selves constitute themselves by the accusation;
the self as they understand it is nothing but the
accusation or the scream.

- Leo Strauss

Enola Gay

I should have never been powerful.
I should have never let aileron
touch the sun.
I have wounded violence itself;
birthed, in flash and horror,
a new primitive age.

I have plunged my
countrymen deep amid the
darkest and most brackish tides,
here where the light
won't touch.

I gaze from the border
at the glow.
In agonized and elegiac note,
war has divested all art
for grimmer techne,
and in the shadows of men,
in that then distant land of dawn,
I have buried what made my life worth living.

II

Knowledge has withdrawn
back to its old springs:
the surfaces of stones,
etchings of stelae, shadows
of uncounted days
cutting chiaroscuros
over the tawny cotton grasses.
In a world of numbers
is hidden an amniotic mind.
How can we know truth?
There is only the conspiratorial,
the serpent clipping the heels of dogma, somewhere,
moving in widdershins,
performing a rapine ceremony
where the essence
of the common man's common wealth,
the secret,
vanishes undignified.

III

        if you were honest
you could, too, see how
you drive
in equal measure against that ache.
Here I can leave a
space   to allow
you to   place
your own grief
and its names, faces, tones,
rhythms; into this gravesite,
colorless but for your memory.

Come, deny yourself little.
Involve yourself however your
redolent comforts demand:
the spice of skin,
lopsided flicker of hospitals,
the night's silence
above newly created absence.
You have denied what is real beyond thought;
the agora I walk, the threadbare menagerie,
will cry for recognition.
Fill me (you must)
in our shared garden
of loss.

Judas Iscariot

Having slaved, and risen,
the milling echoes have fallen away from
my life, and the present vestments
have drawn me toward the monolith;
the promise of surety.
And it is gone.

Betrayed, sold to the passing
revolutions of a promiscuous madness;
a lurid scene where I
once held faith like
a razor in my pocket.
I sold my last protections
to buy off death.

This phantom, burdened
by the visions of city rising,
the huddled and exposed on misery's
altar, commiserates with the repeated
agony of the malnourished spirits
fed to the engine.

Metonymic screams ring through
the concrete ligaments of the camp.
Whoever followed their savior out
has left no words for us at all.

We no longer rise, in our love,
from nature to harry masks
and cite spirits that attest the human genius.

When man becomes the project of
the aliquot, the subject and not the flower
of arm and eye, he has no patrons
in the rushes of changing light.

The craftsmen are always ugly,
always grafted to their engines of artifice,
and abstracted into the rotting God. The fulminating
noise of sacred jism overbears and leaves no gardens,
no keepers, and no secrets.

Each man is an underworld, confined
to the shouting roads, begging imprimatur
in the gap where, once, a proud
darkness vivisected font and frontier
and allowed him to push into himself.

Forcing the safeguard

Run the razors at the border
of myself,
like the sheer
whistle through the chaff;
cut through community.
Allow darkened doors to
aggregate like freckling skin.

Every brutal edifice and
juvenile seed twining
sadly through the epinastic
microcosm of these fences,
the city sutures;
every pool of blood
stretching coquettishly into
the security spotlights
of silent municipal buildings;
augurs our liberty.

Withhold nothing from us,
indulge the excesses
curling moral bones inward,
porous, gout-afflicted
as the wind filters us to naked utility.

Suit

Foremost and definite figure:
the hungry priest is clothed
in coarse night-skin vestments demurring
his naked monstrosity
in the street lamps.
A navy-smattered hierodule.

My birth may be a wound
that won't heal, but his is
a trapping, bound to the abattoir,
ready for others to suffer on his behalf.

The dark and genteel spiral mind
of the collective urban sprawl,
curled like hot glass over
annealing traumas, in him suggests resilience.
He borrows many hands
to command his teeth.

John Henry

Joyroar emanates out of amylase cloud, consuming;
five figures breathe in their champion —
gollyrocking mimicry passes mutually between them.
The bloom of a laughing flower, with the stormiest
figure at the heart, pure power,
drunk with the roiling will
of driven steel, fastened to the earth.

He holds, for their ignorance and frailty,
the jaws of the city, peers inside the machine,
bleeds in its gullet, watches age accrete, precipitous,
as his time quickens,
pulls him faster towards rest.

He knows, fearlessly, this concession;
looks to till the garden with agonal hammer,
unsure if life really does return;
does his best to save all, to suffer smiling,
to hold his men together.

In the windows beyond, down the street, a child
is crying on the floor.
He has a rough life.

Payaso

In a cruel age the
study of joy is left
to the serious –

a gamboling ear traipses the
street-tables:
worn stones; in a stream of
tinkling bonhomie,
twilight blooming, warm as the air
and wind-touched in its rivulets
of laughter, curved like graffiti.

Minute pleasures gathered in
the flow of wandering spirit, ephemeral harlequin of
vespers, viand jester
plucking music out of forgotten fork –

small fare.
Sorrowful prose and lyric
is stamped in heavy lettering
on the brow of the wanderer;
these gadabouts either
sad or insane.
A lone fool carries
the ragged sack of happiness.
A spirit pure, hated by few
a dying animal to be
written out of the page.

City Salvage

In the timbre of its complaint, sounding
through the stifling fingers of buildings,
the horn echoes, in me, blind
motion. Pure release velocity
held in empty hips marching over the wind.
I am swept through the eddies.

Where is my doubled and sympathetic image
in this territory of sheer surface,
unyielding tympans of deafness,
signs of the great America and its bottomless hunger
for beauty to display?
Elsewhere.

I speak for the concrete and
wrought iron altar in my desire
for the old ignorance, the venerable
and simple hatreds
blooming in the rush of life,
like countless hearts under
the earth.

I cannot be granted familiarity
among these stones and choking cromlechs,
cattle-prod depots and engines of heaven.
These towers, beyond putrefaction,
form an acrostic of the absolute.

It is a world of pinprick and refuse.
Darkened curbs like
rain-scorched jaws that swallow those

without faith, anchored to
chintz decays, potted lives,
empty windows filled with the raving gnash of the
bereft.

In this land, composed of
petty masters with treacherous
servants,
agony, agony, agony precedes the
final denial of fealty to the Whole.

There is no freedom but dominion.
What do we pursue but the back ache
plexus of another's head shoved beneath?
The mass is a mountain.
The mass is a vista.
I am alive in my distinction.

Tableau

The city's mad language of lights
shakes with septic grace.
The empty display of transitory
shuffle, gowned,
bedridden,
tied to the brick,
suffused in priapic voltage,
held in fiery skin; these macro signs that
horrify amid gentler shine flickering on,
off, cycling colors lighting, intermittently,
the damp, mirroring street.

There is no new country,
all things are enwombed in this
siren lattice of prurient
hands.

In the hopeless hours,
the dying culture dreams of vacancy and admission,
of a self with no facets
like the machine noise of an electric vessel
enveloping the planet,
no language,
no body,
no sails,
pure heavy horizon.

Shambling

The man of weeds
accretes city grit in
his fingers, plumbing ligneous
foramen to gather his
aluminum, to purchase reprieve from the
joint-itch of poverty.

That subterranean bird,
ill-equipped for the stones,
mangled by telluric trysts,
is mythic in its faith beneath abundant ugliness.

I'll say what builds under the
soft tissue clothing teeth:
this is crisis, and its meanings
are the absence of the ark;
the shrinking of life's gardens;
our written skin become wizened bark
corroded, spun from sickly soul beneath.

The grim enamel scream,
like birds unleashed in the absence
of sunrise,
is received in the raw scrape
of panicked conscience.
You hear it.
There are no more obelisks;
no such thing as indigo.
The end of language circles
the border of severance.

We are the lasting, pitiful end.
We are born in the corpse of a titan,
carrying small fruits, stiff cloth,
harsh chemicals.
Witnessing the cessation of the common man's
dignity in the face of silence.

Chintz

Holding court in home's intimacy;
this body, where loneliness
pools in halogen bruising,
as wires twitch
like the grass disturbed by insects,
this woman, gowned in her shapelessness,
metastasizes into
a frail and entangled nucleus
of the environs:

her dust permeates the fabrics,
rests like gutterkissed flowers
after rain, saturated beneath the vanguard arachnids
in small ogive corners
illuminated by the
jeremiad of electric seizure,
lone television gazing in all directions;
lights cast on this street:

a rapine portrait of an
interior war where I can hear,
muffled, a clarion.

Hierodule

My hands, gifted with shadowed fuzz
from the neon assault of bars,
are twitching hawkish around
the sure circling of these lighted districts.
Garrulous women strut,
muted in the time of absence,
glittermasked, running from shadow to sky,
where they disappear.

Those frail moments of real passage
are the vanishing cut of abandonment,
as desolate as nude trees, flooded nests;
sprinting with unsure purpose
across my body mirrored
in this black, shrinking field. I know
I am on the periphery
as they give themselves away to ruin.
To be marked. To collect meaning written by
vulgar finger.

Homunculus

There is nowhere left to build.
Passing through the beast's glottis
is the whole noise of steel and glitter
metastasis in its corpse, clotted in the corners,
hidden from light's unkind definition.

Men imitate this god, swallow,
become futile, lie flat.
The brow ridge above the mocking
grin of death
is a taut windsail of this assemblage:
veins filled with sound
eyes filled with quiet
voice the cry of something slaughtered.

The architecture presses hard upon
a mass I once considered life.
A mass so grand and vibrantly at play with dawn;
whose faces reflect the scarred and forlorn brass
of lover carved into monument,
deprived of gentle touch.
Whose serpent soul is coiled in fearful clutch

and caging a nameless weight.
Breath like finch leap
carries my currents. Fed muscle
and flesh
grow anxious crop beneath
the bulwark for
air, rain, grime, cut.

Some wicked omen
is writing itself out
in the alley rows,
forming the symbol of crowning
collapse.
The beat, slowly, of force,
grows and grows and grows

Reuptake

Make me judge behind these walls,
placid grins of the masks
of the crowd, the swell of inured unthinking;
shifting ribbons of the spiritually dead;
increments of life's unslowed birthing;
And I will instruct.

The prowling want that echoes in every face,
tongues untouched by honesty, to be
plucked and scattered in the marriage of
frenzy and idle selfishness; I want exposure
to bring them clear and crying into the world.

If I am lonely, it is the loneliness of vision.
If I am callous, it is due to the flagellate
play of their love, to higher virtue unransomed.
I am not isolated, I am only
willing to acknowledge the machine.

The Surgeon

He sees the cut before he makes it,
between hunger and the itch.
Through city vein, aluminum cans in hand,
he carves the hill,
mousing, breaking, throwing

(his whole body is a lance;
attached is the principle of
scission).

Mad, carves up the beast to buy,
once, for a moment,
the salve of the universal.

Syringe

In this lot lies a
small monument, memory of power
evenly issued, anchor of the soul,
rejoining white kiss of the spirit.

I see them, each a
derelict, empty after ceremony.
Filling gutters, memory of communion
in tracks, arms; a spine to cut
the living world.
A bottle to feed it rain and youth.

Age

The crook of night environs
this corner and its ghosts;
draped tarpaulin over thin frame,
hollow people under metal limb.
These new Cartesian men,
in bloodless extension,
hobble in sickening skin
by the mission houses.

I had not even tasted the sweet vines curling
in nude abandon, unpruned,
where thorn and crook named
the futile curves of body
that are blind to utility
(spiritually myopic with the terse joy of the child)
before I knew these old assemblages
with bodies like impost.

This is a den of amputees,
reaching nowhere,
treading scar,
no longer able to hold the young
or show my body its use.

Lament

Around the cancers of
the tented enclave,
men here give their lives
to the dropper,
reading scars under devout habit,
scribbles of unmeaning track,
babble against sense —
I might carve and
winnow my skin
to be like canyons
yielding to the weeping sun
and feel them in
their horror, weakness,
victimhood.
See life as it must be.

Flag

The tender burn I can feel
assailing attenuated nerve,
back of the eye, is one of a million
constituent fires lit in flashing array.
The colors are a poem that hides
its reading, teases the unconscious.

The slinging of unfathered
images, inscription of signs
with infinite regress,
positing the symbol
as the nation; the wave of empty
reason flutters through the
epithelium of every fixture
tying the subject:

its titterings,
peaceful twitches of grass,
the twilight hum
of ripening summer,
the safety of a lover's hands,
a dog tripping over a thing
it loves;
these absent simplicities
hang between the definite.
Our language of comity is the wind
in the gallows.

inside out

An electric scream calls out against
these numbers,
a scrupulous and huddled hydra trading
calumny among its heads.
The shriek redoubles back into the
utterer, rubbed raw and numbed.

The placid backs of huddled fauna seated
in wood form a wheel of counter-insinuations.
Diametric sins spin in a corolla
like a child casting mud into the rain;
against bark,
into the sky.

I can see, buzzed,
through a mirror
that cuts away and
inverts my image:
another spoke in the wheel
of iniquity and the meld of this mill
for language.

Collide,
desultory crowd huddled against
the languid chill that
empties from every unlit
corner of the city; before us,
anomaly
man raging, in rags, brought out
of Gerasa and striking the road
with us;
vigilant phantoms and the great victim
of the body, the champion
and lowest of us.
His beastly madness;
our wary break from his path
as he carves the graves
in like prowl.

I crawl through the matted
comb of towers, each equal
fixture holding star and road to the
stagnant body of the sleeping Earth,
rutilant with void,
an empty mirror
below my renewing vigil.

Where was I among these figures?
Cruel crowd without a master,
unhindered by the highest blade of sky,
vulnerable to our building
rages; sprawl of mutual blindness
in the new waste of febrile grim.

Dementia

I see through the window, cutting evening with light,
an old woman holds court for absence.
Foremost of the lost and mad, spinning,
investigating the foot-worn furrows and dates,
she grasps her menagerie of domestic talismans:
a worn kitsch collective bulwark against anxiety.

Something is missing. The telephone stares in silent
anxiety,
Oppressing, with pregnant amnesia, the mind under
harsh light.
Eyes glaze over the dustless cross on the wall and
glass-cabinet talismans.
The living room averts its eyes from the calendar's
naked absence.
The fridge hums the one-tone lull of the dates.
Pacing through a gestalt body, checking functions,
spinning,

The fuzz of a loose-jointed now keeps spinning.
The heavy musk of rot from the stairs induces a
nameless anxiety.
There is no assistance or saviors written in the dates.
The sudden burst of cold has the rhythm of the light.
In between the moldy food, the gelid plastic, searching
for absence,
the mind cannot strum the crossed wire symbols of
these talismans.

The talismans, which once were bound by memory, are
just talismans,

and each appears disconnected, isolated, before the
eye's spinning.
An object that once meant "rest" now holds a symbol
for final absence.
Some familiar stasis among this disarray should cure
the anxiety,
but its pieces lie smashed, rolled away, filthy, under
coldhearted light
in a ransacked kitchen whose tile bedding is as
uniform as the dates.

Old fetid calendar, blackened fruit: bananas, oranges,
dates.
No notes or reminders under wicker basket, a talisman
of continence, the clock, a talisman of continuity, the
spoons, of light.
In their reflection is an uprooted image, inverted,
spinning.
Funny little reminders in the passage to bliss from
anxiety
and the forgetting of self, and hunger, and absence.

What once were caring hands are touches of absence.
What once provided sustenance is not here to mark
the dates.
What once hummed words of comfort proffers silent
anxiety.
What once cleaned the broken glass has abandoned
the talismans.
What once was a tether of memory has left this home
spinning.
What once had the weight of life is incomparably
light.

The reek of the absence overpowers the talismans.
How many dates have passed in this spinning?
This anxiety will not be debrided by the morning light.

Riot

It is two monsters;
the many-limbed and loud,
hairy, amorphous eukaryote
nervous with hatred and in constant aplomb
with the phantom between, the loveless
magnetism that draws the noise,
smothers the lone and soft individual
in grapeshot bursts.

The dyad observes itself. Its emergent
and diaphanous matter
that hangs the cells together, limping,
extravasated, is in dialogue with the form,
the actual heft, the clumsy push of bend
over waist forming
autofellatio in
convolving spiral.

Who among you will appeal to me for forgiveness?
When may I stand beneath the eye of this great
assignation
and behold myself beatified?

Meet

I fall in at The Sunrise
under warm glow giving
agonized shape to the
refugees from advancing blue.

Within an ignorant calm before the
twilit office, I abandon
myself into the company
of strangers, become the fabric,
bludgeoned into sin.

Beyond myself, truly, and in proximity:
the holly-headed Fool, a moralist despite
himself.

"I watched someone die," I say,
Having endured inuring pleasantry
"I can't even think straight."

'I believe you.'

"I can't stop replaying it in my head, over
and over, off of that bridge."

'We have lost childhood's greatest luxury, to
forget, that's why we are all here.'

"You think we're walking around on the
planet to forget."

'No' he laughs toward the room 'That's why

we're here, in this bar'
Someone cries out in triumph; the hours keep
turning.

"I've been out drinking, and the streets are
teeming with homelessness and
schizophrenia, and I can see miserable yeast-
life growing through the backlit windows
everywhere else. All this misery and
degradation; people gratifying their bodies"

'You want to take away pleasure? It's our
last possession. There is nothing else but the
labor altars'

"Allowing them to behave this way is what
brought us here."

That mirrors are grinning
He sighs
'They are cowardly, fearful, and unprincipled,
but they
desire good as best they know how.'
'For this, they ought to be saved.'

"They want to eat each other"

'Only because, like you, they don't see
themselves in their brethren.'

"You're an idiot. You can't look out there
and tell me that these are good people.
Everyone preying on each other and whoring

out everything they have until there is nothing left."

'Ah I see. Ignorance is your friend, and shame is his dagger. No wonder you are so bereft, if you won't except that real truth can come from play, from the ramifying language of our common mind. How, then, can you love people, who are nothing but individual vortices of this chaos, placed here, knowing nothing, wanting in all directions, without structure, with love, between reason? All this agony and we might be spared if you stopped demanding that life fit itself into some ewer.'

His glower, a mirror of firelight in dusk.

'Should others suffer for your comfort?'

The venomous fire bleeds
behind my sternum, numbing,
blurring my definition,
finding pores in the veil,
building religion, calling with the agony
of stone held solid.
There: specific and tender;
I absolve against the border
of myself, what world I can carry.
I repeat foolish laments and atrocious exaltations
for the stitches of death's distinction
in the real.

Grifters cling in clay
misery to each other circling,
empty of old clothing,
unable to undress, to
be seen in the shape of their ends.
Even skin is their symbol,
pulled to tighten the body
for interment.

Eleventh Hour

I'm drinking open-doored; the
treading night air over raw scrape.
Behind are the laughing shadows, my skin stung
by the brinespray of their noise.
Prurient trading carries between masks.
They are as invulnerable as disease.
My own control over the unlit
hollows behind my face fades,
drives me out, makes me sick and cowering
beneath the glass.

What is loosed, what they can see,
are the merciless digits marking extreme hour.
Crawling from the safeguard into the open
sin of evening, where nothing watches,
monstrous hands prey toward a sickened want.

I can finally grasp the body of the serpent,
the ethereal dark that saturates all figures
in our blind flower womb hidden
beneath the petals; not yet able
to hold their beauty against the nourishing sun,
such closing surrounds us.

Who will be sacrificed,
bursting the overripe skin
of sameness and enervation,
held up to my judgment in the bitter
mass writhe of the selection?
I wish to cut the throat and bring
the harvest, we have indulged too long.

Sudden Bliss State

In the liquor I feel it,
rouge popinjay, a world of plants skinless,
point of nourishment, black,
tart rind, minute
pluck and tongue-shove,
juice ballast, trove
of remnant,
swallow, consummate, flavor-fade,
crush.

The reprieve of flowing
matter, night air the warmth
of breath,
an exchange of mouths
saying "you."

Written on the verso,
there were leaves of sadness,
horror, and joy.
Ahead, in the billboards,
lighting unsure symbols
with exacting sameness,

last halogen Satan.
Exquisite and without referent,
containing all falsity,
knowing what it means to be God's
most perfect creation.

In an epoch of
strange bedfellows I
have as mine the common
mother, the woman bathed
in satin moon, the orange blooded
midnight, love from the overwrought,
the scoundrel,
the peccant.

In halogen island I
gaze toward this emergent
mistress, somewhere above. In
my dejection, the
forlorn and hungry vermin
of desultory glow,
spines craning in sex,
eyes pained in
recursion,
are doubled for me.

The mother would say she knows me -
her place in the Earth, among the vacant
trees, islands without birdsong;
if she rose here to greet the disparate children,
she would recognize me best.

And beyond recriminations that sound,
like symphony cannons, to evoke
a triumph that has no front,
the hands of nature would fold
against the tender fields of skin
and recoil from the othering mouth.

She would know that I would keep
these men from suffering
were there not
this destruction from unfurling,
explosive molt;
this criminal bitterness in turnabout
for my rejection;
this, love's seed lying burnt in my honest
heart
where darkness shifts the garden wall.

Between the long hopes and marcescent pleasures
of the tendril crowd
are the lonely shades
of dreamers and suicides.
The suicides gathering pity,
and the dreamers, contempt.

Opening despair's longtooth doors
is an art of emptiness,
where each of the murine grapes,
restored to manhood, may find himself blooming
in an isolate vine, away from sunlight,
quietly bursting.

Why peer under the altar when the poor
march on quietly? When the soft sounds shot
into bedsprings will be held until the sun returns?
They might find themselves there, suffering
as well, one more victim of a disease only
a mass can sustain, where each dies alone from
mutual unacknowledgement.

The drawn shades of that apartment
are the closed soul bracing
against the wild bite of the blinded;
the genuine savage that skulks the curtain.
Something like a tryst inside —

Here, a consonant friction.
The kyphotic pharmacologist
trades his poison tongue
to devise new color
in the sallow-sick recesses
at the heart of you:
a dim   where once resided
a healthy light
that the Domineering physician would have
mistaken for purity.

Moral Contagion

Composing these men is a
perverse effusion of radio poison,
coiling into unified spirit,
souring the bones with permanent weakness;
the ill transfigured into
snapping and schizophrenic hydra.
I've come to know

this distrust in the indefinite
gardens, where all are masked
and tense-shouldered. I too possess
the internecine language of the
warfaring paranoid, dancing the labyrinth
sexualities, exploited.

You fear it, and do not deny.
This clash and threat, collision shock
of wills unclothed of accident; snakes in orgy.
In one and in all my hate is a rhyme.

Fall

The night air
with its colors and sense;
all are hung about my mouth
in my tripled regress seeking
withdrawal into my
saccharine, brachiating watch of the fringe roads.
My nerves strike outward in endless campaigns
that fade between the colored islands
and lone homosexuals seeking private dramas.

Shock falls away with a light sweetness,
blood drifts in its raucous way - my body a drunk
legion
your body the Earth to which I wearily return,
infantile,
uncaring,
and laughing with every muscle; thought
and tongue searching to bury in you.

Dream

I keep you so something
beyond the black static texture of ego
moves without my wanting,
sometimes;
so double eyes can
examine my life,
sing its ramified diseases,
see that it behaves.

At a point
deeper than feeling, beneath
will, in
habit,
passive,
ugly,
with smell,
tickle,
ease,
habit,
heft,
custom:
I can retreat and be just the same;

harp-pluck neuron
brushes its naked back against
the warm refuge in the penumbra.

These animals in the home of dawn,
possessed of live mass;
twilit, liminal flowering of air flux, heaviness,
ripening.
Together they crest,
burning what was gathered in the day;
convolve, sin, and join,
denuded of will.

The patron that holds them together:
the lash at their back
compelling them
to wander between
the warehouse and machine.
Now free to hold (twitching, lonely)
their neighbor
in common refuge from
daylight's god of misery.

The Samurai

When I knew you as dynamic elm
attached to the phantom name
that draws thin, grey faces from your grave,
I imagined I saw a woman:
golgi body soul; that labyrinth
in and in and in through engines of life
to the sweet delirium of being.
A tool for my suicide.

But you were at war,
in your lone strides gathered,
in the arbor crowd of
real lies and lecherous harms,
forever guarded as you danced in striking range;
unloved, unknown,
carving yourself into a manageable whole.

Cathedral

The collective sound, the
abjuring choke of breath before
a stifled cry, accretes in bare matter.
Men conform to the naked trees and
iron gates in the genuine poses of mourning,
unaffected and bereft.

The church in its austere nightclothes is steward
to the last supplicants murmuring a haunting-
language of suicide. This mass
is a languid body pulsing with the
import of a desperate and viral word,
imploring a god, tasked with crying over loss.

Above them, our dark is reflected
from sky to window to heaven to street
cutting through the shaded color
of these shiftless that are
inuring themselves to the windy rush
of healthy city-blood.

My head carries their secret,
turning through addict obsession
into the strange phrases of agony
in my own breathless flight
from identity.

Love letter

I wanted to love you
beyond rebar fields, in the soil
of the derelicts where
you hide secret musings
and store wild secrets
away from order's blank lattice.

I wanted you, there,
in the privacies of addiction and resentment:
a concave mirror of aluminum;
the lambent electric nightscapes
of nerve-fire that trace
insomniac rivers
and guide me through this unconscious procession
into freedom.

I wanted all men in the broken fields of
street-vein, vacillating ruin and repair,
to grow
with me in play and in song.

The silence out here is
heavier than my teeth.

Heroine

Hairy-cell sketches of addicts
nod and bend in whorls around
the bowel where I descend,
the impromptu chapel where hierarchy
displaces one servant with chemical hands;
who eases the lank and crooked
poverty of an inconclusive Mass.

What the crowd knows to be the last,
most monstrous God kneels, itself,
beneath the virile, aging charity of
this woman and her simple symbols
of amnesty, hung in their necks.

She, the rare flower of love,
inveterate in the
grid of iron fields where recrimination
blooms.
I, forgotten, already, under the sudden
and desultory sketch of rain
that fell from her voice.

Outside, in the world
beyond the yet unsculpted wind
that fondles all flowers,
I have no faith in my own reception.
These fragile and sable borders of
individuality, when ventured
beyond, reward me with suffering.

Where is the love object,
the sweetness undressing me
with futile damage, scratching, tugging me
beyond myself into her?

Only the disparate lines,
the rough ugly
of the souls allowed to
sow impulse and accrete pollution.

When I knew her, she was air,
and my voice carried toward her
over canyons, scars of earth
made empty, where she resided.
Whipping bright angel shale as temperature
shifted, as hue of wind grew out
in rhythmic bloom from the fission.

I knew her, and she became weight,
slumping me in a constant pressure pull
into dirt, crevasse, sepulcher. Twisting me.
Delighting in how I reneged myself.

I knew, as I know now, the monster I became,
was she: roving yonic alleys. Making me
foul and cretinous, asking for damage.
Pushing me to transgress,
mocking the noble thing I could have loved.

I

The whole city
is tugged in the half knot
of one slipshod, impecunious shadow directed gargling
through the moon.
The last creature, the giftless and festering child,
runs darker than the evening
beyond the tent district into his last abode,
empty of love.

II

a mendicant asks for a cigarette,
is the vine encircling another,
becomes pliant at the feet of the city;
she hugs him as he listens,
he is small between lashes;
the last singer toward the world
with its doubled scorn, dampening
with great and fragile waters.

There in the rain, he sees himself,
at last, in the mirror of vice
surrounding him, devoid of romance, true.

Cathedral

Trekking to the head, toward the mouth
of the spirit, bleeding
through the massive agonized city.
I am the transverse scar.
Both hidden, even as primordial
and psychic as we are,
in the demure nudity of night.
The crowds in play still rush with
vascular purpose under
anti-color sky.

I cut through the last crowds, asleep beneath
the stone figure of the church mission.
These final stragglers before the
vacant roads —
where we are left in the empty with hungers
for which we
have yet no names.

All is a roar, distant, reflected figures caper in
a black narthex window,
opaque as the master
in his inverse presence
among the mass of the verminous.

No bells sound.
All to suffering and their ends, the silent
king removed,
meal of madness and tree beneath all fates.

Meet

A man vacates his bowels in the street –
a mad animal of protest,
portrait of indecent foramen
kept closed to death.
This child of the last empire,
burdened with
futures not yet actual, forces yet
unexpressed, as we, too, are still playing the
game of age as the
dense void of potential inside us
gains limbs.

'Without that furtive and selfish appetite, we
don't leave the space others need to choose
to be better than themselves.'

"You're really fucking naïve."

He deflects the blow. Crowning himself with
the impish mockery of a man without
possessions. He makes me long for gardens
he must know.

'Naïveté is necessary. Without that child's
spirituality you can't bridge concern for your
fellow man.'

"There is nothing 'spiritual' about the
beatings and depredation around us."

'Every man has a spiritual impulse.'

"Spiritual. They take their fear of death,
their need for control and order, and abstract
it so that they can believe that these horrors
won't happen to them. This they call
spirituality. Some egoistic acknowledgement
of what lies outside."

'It's almost romantic.'

"Being blithely stupid doesn't help; everyone
is selfishly harming everyone around him,
everything he gains is a privation for
someone else, and they go on without once
considering how much suffering they cause
in this wasteful game."

'Everything conceived in spring is born in
winter, and everything born in winter is a
steward of rebirth. You don't think that
living is a heroic act? You seem to believe
that you're the first to consider death as
admirable. That no one you saw ever
considered anything but the rote instinct of
devouring.'

"That's all it is for these people! They cling
to life out of base animal cowardice. They
disgust me. Walking through all this misery,
feeling it and turning away because they
can't confront it. They exist by default,
numb through denial."

His laugh was the brush of snow off the head of a child.

'You're one to talk about being a coward. You can't even look at your fellow man in the way you want them to see you. How will you face something like death? You'd need someone to leave the light on for you.'

If only he knew.

Underneath the network of raised urban artery
I can hear the sighing heft of the organism ringing
through the absent bodies and headlamps;
as devoid as the warmth and harmony
in the collective meaning of these
isolate icons;
the malaise of the city, the horror presented with
a shame better than honesty;
striking pillars that refuse
collapse.

I would summit, just as empty, if
I weren't trapped, haggard,
awry in rivers flowing slow,
like the rot taking the gutter food,
permeating it with conquering flags
of the natural world,
building a cannibal forest
that I carry beneath hewn,
unlit skin that runs cold
in the premonition of a rebellion of
life against mounted stone spine.

The last choke of urban meaning
reaches the telluric heaven in its roots.
The symbols of pure division multiply.

The map has come alive, its
torpid growths are gutted in
vastation;
the cells beneath give way to the
cancer of man's understanding,
railing through,

shattering each of the endless limbs,
setting distant fires,
moving, extravasated, in infinite orgones
chewing space.

The play has long concluded
its protracted life
of still nudes on the
stage -
dance becomes rest, rest
becomes trope, and
death occurs without notice.

Blood on the astragal

the transom above the tenement door
is browned and webbed
by derelict arachnid.
The wood in its coquettish rot
is the revealing symptom
of our bare and comfortable dissembling
of decline.

The gnats hover
in monkish grace,
courting with genteel nudge;
the scampering vermin
are civilized
under the grim decay;
the tender letters of paraphernalia
left scattered in the anxious absorption
of despair are the tangible vacancy
of voice.

The sun has exited,
and a train
quenches its sound furtively.
I possess that blindness.

Dragged through the air's sexual
befouling,
I am the last shudder
in the expanse —
the serrated tandem of
needle and engine falls behind me.
I am lost to the heart,
or some organ of
needful discharge,
adrift in sleeping cargo,
waiting for one final operation.

You've come to realize
too late
that this is
a game of long horizons;
machine axles channeling the
allayed, oft-shorn
edges of the bloodbath
through which you move

Frumpent and scarred pale from
each day's plexiglass psychosis.
Every man lugs his disobedient body
through the prison.
Every harm-heavy tendon of the sleeping
dead stretches, warring
against the loneliness of the roaring signal
that constitutes a mating scream from
the collective conscious.
Here to build bollards
against history.

The Rat

The furtive shame of the crawl between
unlit, sheer brick-face, animates the scavenger
in the alley over which he is master.

Ensconced by the rain-sodden refuse,
between the contemplative junkies
stupefied by the ground, cringing,
picking with twisted joints,
He exits the sure lights.

He grasps a precious item, blinded,
squealing, pulling into his home,
the space where nothing stays.
Suppression follows, suffused with the cold grains
of night on groin, matted scruff, the crying; just a
little
nails on gorget,
clothing his famine songs
just hold please
just a little just
stop
raw offal
just yes hold a little
just there
close just
gnawing wounds that scar inside
just a little there
yes just there the lament of joints
(quick breath in the heart)
on the concrete where the sky's tears
can kiss the curled

coming-through-the-skin
flowers of paper
yes like dresses and coquettish gifts
just please for a moment

He scurries,
a trail of wreckage is furrowed.

Hostile Architecture

The warble of a schizoid wave
crests the city, florid with
the soft physician's light of dawn.
Razor-wire sundries are surmounted,
nicks on thieving arm form
heavy constant anchors
in this last headspace,
the true outskirts.
Among rags I join
the restless crush of
impost; free, bit by bit,
from the abstractions
of ego and, forward, carry
with violence toward
my simplest state.

Straightjacket

This woman will die by suicide, or in obscurity,
but not both.
This city is her wings; beyond her mind
and its shouting,
I can step through
and engage the illness.

She is famous, but she is scorned.
She skips through maddening fields
but holds hands with the rivers.
Her lover is the full-bodied giant of life,
who abuses her daily.
She is deathly afraid, and lusts
after death.
She is between the pillars of sighing,
its heights and its fanging plinth,
splayed open in total nudity
to crash the feast of her humiliation.

Brawl

This street fight is a body forgotten
in amorous play, heavy and naked
under the swinging, tensing wrists.
Two men pushing, probing
the strange and like flesh
undone under cotton.

When they rise in their waves
of childish epithet,
a note sounds above the tremolo,
the cracking lingers on one of the
lovebirds, places him dazed
at the empty border of street,
litter, and vacant shelter.

There, darling;
if you sat and held like
a heavy breath that vector
from the throat,

clear and sharp
as a headwound,
you could be dampened
by the fine string that dangles,
close as your ear.
A signifier
beyond which hums
mute beauty.

The Lord is carrying the
stamen intertwined with the feather of a
crow,
openly weeping,
and grimacing long-haired
at the flowers,
sparse, abuzz,
singing with their warm sway
in the grass-jig of subterranean
beetle.

The raucous columns
of the highway bridge are
silent at his passing.
By the river, a violinist plays and a child wails in
tandem
offering the sound of
light-starved velocities of sadness
and the sweating lunacy of
schizophrenics in withdrawal.

The suicide

I

I divide –
pinned gaze to the lacey
buttress of flying
bridge, legless, armless,
orthogonal to myself,
paralyzed under dark;

there, lurched, imperiled
on all borders,
land and air, abscissa and ordinal, motion and
stillness,
seen and invisible,
life and death, stretches limbs
out in last symbol
of crossing,
frees me, where, now, the figure leapt, there never
was.

II

(If only all wounds had this absent
signifier where breath is caught beneath breath
in a thudding choke)

catches, I am loss, pure, stretching and splintering
into the
wind

(here he is stripped bereft at

death's nude gaze, agonized by the real limit of
himself, alike)

something I could have held,
beyond me, a world I cannot know

(and razed by disaster, here is the grave of the
last detractor of evil's sharp edicts)

The cage of present yanks
its hooks on all axes.
I feel the prison, scorched steel
cerebrum of suicide,
veins desperate to tear free;
let the city surrender its metal,
this river its corpses,
this bridge its rivets, this town
its vagrant circling around absent light;
free me from the agonized march!
All static repetitions fall,
let me feel again.

Cold will clear the garden
populated by the last feathers dislodged
from unclaimed earth;
sterile under the vanity of treacherous gibbous.

The revival of the spirit,
from that horror, from the surface from
which no birth harmonizes
with electric call, will grant me stillness, respite,
atop the torpid grave
that is nourished, lovingly
as I.

Train

I'm finished, the last choked twinge of surfactant
walls lost in slough, my head in a spiraled
darkness of this many-steepled tomb, the
oven of breath's enterprise with fuel of the soul.
I'm looking for the heavy light.

I want to wake into something peaceful,
which I inhabit and shelter
in my limbs, ligaments, neurons,
squamous and electric networks
wetted with fresher blood.
The city-body languid, untroubled,
public in the noble sense;
not harried and anxious, populated by the sentry
lights
of desultory buildings,
where each lamp is a woman
refusing to undress.
I want to feel warm again.

Tremble, lines of rage.
Echo the song of
intention from the body nexus,
indignity that I feel
carried, won
from this distant ravine.
Hidden, dim-lit by
forgotten mental architecture –
the rest and crystallization
of the spirit.

I hear it
without gravity, from the
tempest where I may reclaim
my own meaning:
the iron track is painted with sound.
Bright wrath bursts the machine in slow motion.
I'm ready, I've traveled downward;
the cherished son not yet grown,
choked in the underbrush,
meeting the steel altar to be given over
in atonement.
This heavy carrier:
into a wound, into emptiness,
where I may refill;
to forgive the damned and wounded horror
exposed by this horn - song of a luminous
redemption.

A force pulls me out.

They carried me like the sun into the
last rest, beneath vision;
an urban valley accosted
by the motion of the wind:
hands of a persistent
sculptor trying to mold this sorrow
into dance and synchronicity with
the seedling life passing above.

I as hollow and airy as the disowned hands
and titters of this family, fording me across
the sluggish time they inhabit.
Holding me curbside,
I see, for the first time, in their eyes,
how to look upwards;
the brush of the real
and necessary ethic.
Here where the shock sets in.

The fire barrel

The remainder   is an
                          infidelity,
black trust:

                          necessary to know the
names of sainted want,   held (at last) in
                          the hand of the mob, stuck

free in our birth, falling

                          away to the sun, gnashing

gossamer
noose, I am   an isolate, august traitor
to these men,
vagrants like all,

                    and suffering in common

          warmth at the base of our need.
          Held no better by love than itch
          or bier. Frightened of the vast
          evening that is my father, an
          austere gaze toward which I have
          cried out in want, rage, recrimination,
          and am received here as a criminal
          equal in the valley of wrong.

Lament

The chill of dawn's hanging
reaches me on the waterfront,
the loose hang deposes weary restlessness –
I am ruled by numbed skin and bell-chime vessel
throb.

A shore where nothing can be followed,
where once wild waters lie comprehensible,
imprisoned, delineated.
Where are the tranquil rapids, above the shifting
purpose of body,
pushing its children where they may be fed, loved,
carried?

I am here to strike stone.
Agonized, impatient, without recompense.

I feel the absence of eyes,
my skin unransomed; the polluted mind
aches from false light and scrip, rambles without me,
blurs the definition between
myself and darkness,
I am among all, and no one.
Why cry out, if my name just echoes against the brick
and plaster?
Where is my pride, huddled
inside our indifferent shelter?

'So you tried to end your life, and they saved you.'

"Saved."

The air inverted over my skin with the heat of a fresh wound.

"Nothing is saved. I'm going to sober up and walk back out there into the abattoir and I'll join that march to the end. My life has only been prolonged."

He raises an eyebrow.

'You have no right to feel sorry for yourself, you are not them; you still had a chance to nurture the fragile things of childhood.'

'I know what you believe. You think, in the cage where we reside, with the heat against us, that we would be saved by passion, instinct, and the ease of ignorance; all of which you believe to be the elements of moral certainty. But the machine of techne is not short on ignorance. We are more ignorant than ever, and we believe that knowing others, knowing ourselves, are simple things, and this is untrue. This is why I tried to make you aware that everything you see is a reflection of yourself. These men helped you, and you still despise them.'

"They probably hoped I'd give them money.
Or they were trying to imagine that they're
not as wretched as they are, that there's
some nobility in them as they sit pissing
away what little they have, slowly softening
into rot."

'So what if they were?
They risked harm to care for you.
And, in any case, they gave you
something that you can never repay:
the possibility of repayment itself.
The continuing chance to be a font
of the good that you feel is lacking.
A light given to others in exchange for
your personal nightfall.'

Sermon

I think you were right, in the end.
Perhaps a false word in a familiar language
is a better comfort to man than his reflection
doubled in the outsider.
But here I am, in all my strangeness
and metaphor, to show that the will,
after pushing through the foreign barrier,
can reach the sunlight.

It is the same when man gazes
on the grim seduction of the night sky,
demasking its auburn twill to show
the fate of all its subjects beneath;
yet still, in his most bereft oceans,
can the most wretched
and poor in spirit be saved.

What have you seen but the frenzied,
unlit grasses of the garden?
Who are you to demand the suicide
of the last beautiful thing?
The firm arms of beauty are
there, just beyond your revulsion,
your ego.
What you have cultivated, what
springs to life in this tamped ground
is truly yours, and you remain
to keep vigil by its lanterns when
need returns from the orgy wood
for refuge.

When I was mad in a sane world,
it taught me to dream,
now a dreamer in a mad world
only I can recognize.
The sublimity of the human spirit
is known in loving it
where one's surety is always under threat,
including the surety of death.

The voyage is already underway,
a new miracle repeats the entrance of light
into the mirrors, ready to receive the peerless
sun and to return its name - I see now the innocence
of this want,
men who reach and wait, stand poised to exit their
darkness,
keep faith in dissolution.
Is it strange that
I return with them to the dawn? I who lost life,
regain anew the surety of day.

Have courage to practice simple wisdoms
in the face of the world;
that loving your neighbor is better
than all sacrifices,
and that in such love you will return
to what you are.

Nursery

Somewhere out in new azure,
in a room holding the sun,
is a cradle stirring
with a slow voltage
unfurling complex instrument
and peal.

She answers the gentle lash of limb;
mending its need,
scouring the loam;
a gardener searching our
common root.

The harmony in the song of her
hands traces the ineffable rhyme
of all touching flesh,
the secret held in common
and given life.

Is this you?
This is me.